CATULLUS: SHIBARI CARMINA

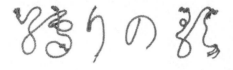

also by Isobel Williams

The Supreme Court: A Guide for Bears (2017)

Catullus: Shibari Carmina

ISOBEL WILLIAMS

CARCANET

First published in Great Britain in 2021 by
Carcanet
Alliance House, 30 Cross Street
Manchester M2 7AQ
www.carcanet.co.uk

A CIP catalogue record for this book is
available from the British Library.

ISBN 978 1 80017 074 2

Cover image: 'Denisse, Whiterabbit and Udo' © Isobel Williams

Book design by Andrew Latimer
Printed in Great Britain by SRP Ltd, Exeter, Devon

The publisher acknowledges financial
assistance from Arts Council England.

For the riggers and the models

With thanks to Belinda Bamber for triage, to Taki Kodaira for calligraphy instruction and to Meredith McKinney for Japanese translation; Jill Ferguson and Violet Hill for Latin teaching; Tristan Franklinos, Stephen Harrison and Stephen Heyworth for tolerating a gatecrasher; the editors of *Envoi*, *The Frogmore Papers*, *Poetry Salzburg Review* and *Stand* where some of these poems were first published. A selection also featured in the Carcanet anthology *New Poetries VIII*.

Trinidadian Creole version of 93 © Jason Anthony Henry 2021.

Photography by Dick Makin Imaging, dmimaging.co.uk.

The Propertius epigraph is taken from S.J. Heyworth's Oxford Classical Texts edition (2007).

libertas quoniam nulli clam restat amanti,
liber erit, uiles si quis amare uolet.

Lovers have no freedom now.
To be free, abandon love.

Propertius II, xxiii

CATULLUS: SHIBARI CARMINA

Shibari (Japanese): binding
Carmina Catulli (Latin): poems or songs of Catullus

These hemp bondage rope characters incorporate *sōsho*,
Japanese cursive script, and say *shibari no uta*
(shibari carmina).

CONTENTS

I

This book belongs to _____

                         … misappropriated
Words glistening raw, vellum exfoliated –
Yours if you want to navigate its folds,
Diving for cargo in the drowned holds.

Tell the teachers dead and alive I'm sorry.
While they were splitting Gaul in three they knew
I'd waste a lifetime waiting for the ferry.

Drop in. Whatever. Take a generous view.
This house dust/book dust will grow damp with tears
If I outlive him, cursed with my hundred years.

I draw Japanese rope bondage (shibari) as an outsider. What I see is created for an audience, with the consent of all parties. No! I am not Miss Whiplash, nor was meant to be.

Catullus was held in emotional bondage by affairs with men and women. The Roman Republic knew nothing of the Japanese archipelago: I use shibari simply as a context.

Shibari ('binding') is derived from the ancient martial art of hojōjutsu. A dominant top, or rigger, ties a submissive, also called a bottom, model or bunny. Performers start with floorwork. The rigger may then suspend the bottom in a sequence of transitions, communicating via breaths and glances. Theatrical elements can include dripping wax on skin (the candles used have a low melting point).

There is a fluid dynamic with a constant flicker of role-reversal. Gorgone, a French star of tying and being tied, describes the paradox of who's really in charge: being a top is about humility, being a bottom is about power.

When tied, Gorgone feels like the golem, the formless creature of clay given shape when the Hebrew word אמת (*emet*, truth) is written on her forehead. The rigger's vision creates her in rope. 'I was nothing and your eyes saw me,' she says.

Thine eyes did see my substance, yet being unperfect; and in thy book all my members were written, which in continuance were fashioned, when as yet there was none of them.
Psalm 139, verse 16

Bless thee, Bottom, bless thee! Thou art translated

Shibari is a form of translation. The top arranges the bottom in a shape he or she could not hold or maybe even attain alone.

In Shakespeare's *A Midsummer Night's Dream*, Bottom temporarily has an ass's head when he is ensnared in Oberon's quasi-shibari public domination of his wife Titania. Translators must try to avoid giving a text the head of a donkey through misreading or doubtful taste, but at least they do no permanent harm to the original. Rope marks on the skin should leave a pleasing pattern but will soon fade.

Side-stepping one problem, my versions here are not (for the most part) literal translations, but take an elliptical orbit around the Latin, brushing against it or defying its gravitational pull.

BELINDA: *Ay, but you know, we must return good for evil.*
LADY BRUTE: *That may be a mistake in the translation.*
       Sir John Vanbrugh, *The Provok'd Wife*

The Poet

Catullus gets under the skin. You suffer with him if you meet him in the schoolroom: all that wounded self and thwarted desire.

He collars you with urgent clarity (what Robert Herrick calls his 'terse muse'). Vital and volatile, elegant and cruel, he is a learned master of poetic form who covers the range: beauty, anguish, tender lyrics, spite; low-life drama, glittery wedding poems, street encounters, sweeping myth; love laid bare in all its moods; and vengeful smutty attacks – a streak of powered-up *Viz* without the good intentions.

Facts about Gaius Valerius Catullus are scarce. His life, or a version of it, is in his poems. Here are some stepping stones to the present:

Circa 84 BC: Born into the minor aristocracy. His father, a citizen of Verona, has a villa on Lake Garda and knows Julius Caesar.

?? BC: Moves to Rome. This is the late Roman Republic, buffeted by rivals grabbing wealth and raising armies. Catullus thrives in a cultured elite. Makes friends and enemies.

Money: Complains about being broke but has private means and a villa near Tivoli. Targets bankrupts and a love rival who can't afford slaves. A book-keeper's eye: 20.35% of his poems include numbers or counting.

Morals: Conflicted. Combines traditional Roman fastidiousness with a racy life which he mines for material, using real names. Targets shaggers, incestuous shaggers, politicians and plutocrats.

Boyfriend trouble: Jumpy and jealous over a sought-after Lord Alfred Douglas type called Juventius.

Woman trouble: Hangs out the love and hate in his excoriating affair with an older married aristocrat he names Lesbia, maybe to highlight her learning: the poetess Sappho was from Lesbos. Sometimes he calls her *domina*, the word a slave would use for his mistress.

If she exists, and as a woman, she might be Clodia Metelli, a politician's wife then widow. Whatever her deeds, trying to live as freely as an unfettered man of the time is enough to get this Clodia a bad rap. The orator Cicero implicates her in incest (with her brother Clodius) and even murder – is her husband's sudden death natural?

Poetry: Writes for a coterie, has an eye on posterity. Targets bad poets. Will be the leading survivor among the neoterics, a polished clique of new poets following Greek models, notably Callimachus who lived about two hundred years earlier. They discard the inimitably weighty Homeric epic for lyrics, elegies and epigrams on more personal themes, and the epyllion, an epic in miniature. Poetry doesn't yet rhyme but Catullus almost does at times, internally and at ends of lines (*angiportis/...nepotes*), building up the music with alliteration and assonance (*ave atque vale; tunditur unda*) and snatches of repetition.

?? BC: Bereavement: his cherished nameless brother dies in the Troad, the region where Troy stood in what is now Anatolia.

57–56 BC: Sampling politics, joins the retinue of Memmius, governor of the Roman province of Bithynia, now north-western Turkey. Is rude about him afterwards. While on this tour, visits his brother's tomb. His lament for his brother (poem 101), full of plangent 'ah' sounds, ends with the lapidary *ave atque vale* (hail and farewell), a monument to the untranslatable and un-updatable.

By 54 BC: Accuses Julius Caesar, who is subduing Gaul and Britain, of lechery, sodomy, letting his chief engineer loot conquered lands, and (possibly the worst in Catullus's eyes) being a pseudo-intellectual. Gets away with it.

Circa 54 BC: Dies – or not – aged about twenty-nine (older than Keats, close to Marlowe). C.H. Sisson's 'the body burnt out by lechery' is not ascertainable. Will influence pillars of the canon, including Horace, Martial, Ovid, Propertius and Virgil, and disintegrate into mere fragments quoted by others.

9th century: A spark – poem 62 pops up in an anthology.

Circa 1300: Crashes through to posterity. A manuscript full of errors, from a time more recent than his, turns up in Verona. It is lost again, but not before being copied to start the chain reaction which draws in Petrarch. Poems 1-60 are short, in a variety of metres, with gaps left by three poems incorporated in the sixteenth century, rejected in the nineteenth. They are followed by seven longer poems, a compact epic and forty-eight epigrams. Scholars debate whether Catullus assigned the poems' order. All I know is that when I rearranged them into boy poems and girl poems it looked like a dog's breakfast.

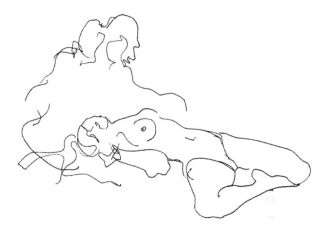

1472: Printed for the first time, in Venice. Catullus scholarship gets going.

1570s: Has been echoed by other English poets, but translation into English kicks off with Sir Philip Sidney and poem 70; pitch invasion starts about 200 years later.

1680: Jean de La Chapelle begins the novelisation of Catullus with *Les Amours de Catulle*, while maintaining that he is writing 'des conjectures Historiques'.

18th and 19th centuries: Catullus and Lesbia are subjects for paintings and engravings which celebrate pretty people in drapery.

1943: First performance of Carl Orff's cantata *Catulli Carmina* for tenor, soprano, chorus and percussion.

1969: C.H. Sisson calls Catullus 'my friend across twenty centuries', an easy mistake to make about someone so compelling but so judgemental.

1972–94: Cy Twombly paints *Untitled (Say Goodbye, Catullus, to the Shores of Asia Minor)*, a vast abstract misquotation from poem 46 which has not shores but *campi* (plains). For a while Twombly calls it *Anatomy of Melancholy*.

2010: Anne Carson's *Nox* (night, also death) makes a reasonable bid for *ave atque vale* dominance with the infinite archaism 'farewell and farewell'.

2019: Let social media judge. 'Catullus: cried during sex' – @ala_Camillae, Twitter

2021: Adding to the tumult, here are my versions of sixty of the 113 poems.

CATULLUS: SHIBARI CARMINA

2

Oh little beak, how Mistress loves
To play with you and guard you in her nest,
Feed your craving with her fingertip,
Sharpen your need, make you nip hard –

She is the glowing core of my desire
But looks to you for flights of entertainment
And a fluttery release, we trust,
To let the tide of urgency subside.

I pray to uncage you as Mistress does
And make the crushing tortures of the soul
Lighter than a feather's stroke.

2 (B)

[?unrelated fragment]
Something something would be
As much relief to me
As sprinting girl in story found
When glinting quince untied the waste of years

3

Break, break, break, love gods and gorgeous people.
Mistress's little beak's been taken –
A consolation she was always petting
For the sheer love of the thing.

It knew Mistress as if she'd hatched it.
Rooted in her lap, it hopped about,
Cheeping just for Mistress.

Now it's submitted to that shady venture
From which no one returns to what they were.
Naughty creatures of the night, how could you –
Scoffing all the beautiful *objets d'art* –
You laid claim to my pretty little beak.

Oh how wicked. Poor little beak.
Now you're to blame for the state of Mistress's lovely
Eyes. Red-raw, tumescent, overflown.

5

Song of Snogs

Open out to life and love with me,
Clodia, and we'll set the regulators'
Hisses at the lowest rate of interest

Suns go down and dawns will come
But once our pinprick light is out
The night will never be for more than sleeping

I love doing this, let's
Take a long position, swell the
Abacus with kisses
M Cxxx
MM CxCx Cxxx
MMM CxCx Cxxx CxCx

And when we've made a killing kissing
Shake the totals to lose count,
Take them beyond the kiss inspector's reach

6

Mr Gold:
Your latest pet must be witless and charmless
Or else you'd confide in Doctor Catullus.

So I'll tell you.
You've picked up some toxic tramp and you're ashamed.

Don't pretend you're filling in time with hand-jobs.
This bedroom's the crime scene –
Reeking of Lynx and sex-club lubricant.

Look, double-dented pillows
And this shuddering, juddering
Bed's got the staggers.

Come clean. That fuck-wasted look
Says you've done something regrettable.

Who is it?
Don't worry about my reaction.

To deal with my responses I make them public
In a disciplined explosion.

7

Stress-testing are we, Mistress?
How many of your tropes in rope
Can be endured before the poet chokes?

Ply me hemp silk jute and tie me
Ichinawa, takate kote,
Futomomo, hishi karada,
Tasuki, kannuki,
Hashira, daruma shibari.
All of it. Semenawa for the burn.

Count the stars that spy on sly
Lovers when the night is ball-gagged –

That's how many of your tight knots and rope marks
Will deliver me beyond madness –
More than a voyeur's torch could spot
Or a jealous sensei take to pieces.

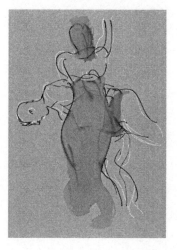

8

In tears again, Catullus. Just get out of bed.
Accept the past and have the loss adjusters in.
Oh, once upon a time you were the golden boy –
When you let Mistress use her harshest ropes on you.
You said you loved her more than all the rest blah blah.
She taught you how to show submissiveness and shame,
Following your instinct, and made you feel big.
The rumour was they even liked you in Japan.

So now she's dumped you and you can't get tied at will.
Don't chase vanilla boys or put your life on hold –
Try Buddhist meditation to endure the drought.

Mistress, get lost. Catullus-san's remade in stone.
He won't beg favours or come sniffing after you.
You'll pine for him now he's not snivelling in your wake.
What's promised for a has-been/never-was like you?
Who's next? Who's going to mumble that you're beautiful?
Who wants to feel the lash and be your slave by right?
Who'll let you kiss him, cut and bleeding in your ropes?

But you, Catullus – you're not even curious.

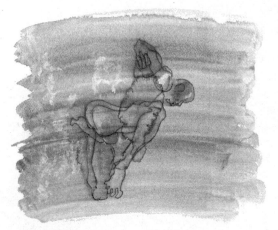

Be prepared

You two – you're my camp
Followers when I want to penetrate
The rim of India, surf-deafened beach-bum paradise,
Or nameless towns for soldiery and rent boys,
Or Parthia to be shot at by the locals.
We'll stain ourselves beside the delta waters
And thrust across the jutting Alps to spot
Caesar's crown jewels – the land of Lederhosen
And the last resort, Britain, where the rough trade
Parades in woad. You're braced for any road
Your luck might roll you down –

So take her this message, will you? Short and sour:

Goodbye. May God bless all who sail in you,
Three hundred Romeos at a time rammed in your
Hold. Forget romance. It's your obsessive
Quest to give them all a hernia.

Don't use my love as collateral.
It died, thanks to your little weakness, like
The elusive flower slashed by the
Combine harvester.

13

We'll have an engorgement party on my sofas
So see you next Tuesday if you're lucky, Fabullus –
As long as you bring the sushi,
A user-friendly sub, some coke, Doritos
And jokes that are actually funny.

Yes, comrade, those are my house rules –
The poet's credit card is frayed at the edges

But I'll repay you with
The essential aphrodisiac,
Mistress's secretions straight from heaven.
One dab behind the ears and you'll comprehend
The naso-genital reflex theory.

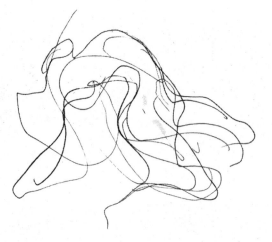

15

Mr Blond, commending
Unto you this day
Myself and the love of my dreams,
Here's the deal:
If you've ever pined
To touch the hem of innocence
Guard him with good grace.

It isn't the crowd that concerns me –
I'm not afraid of your lackeys,
They keep off the grass –
But you and your dick, preying
On boys of all persuasions.
Plant it where you like
Away from your own front door

But if malice or madness
Goad your criminal urge
To offend against my interests
Nemo me impune
Lacessit. You'll pay damages
Splayed out, strung up, receiving
Through your undefended porthole
Radishes for roughage and
Acanthopterygii –
Fish with spiny rays,

Primitive Perciformes
Like you.

16

Sweet

Beware the mighty sodomite face-bandit.
You two batty-boys dishing out lit crit
Insist my kissy-fit verse is Hello Kitty.

Look, being the guardian of what's good
Is work for the poet, not for the poet's works.

Liberation from your taste police
Gives my words a musky allure that can stir

Not just boys but the prick-memory
Of shaggy old ex-shaggers.

So writing kiss poems is an unmanly feat?
First line, repeat. XX

Mr Blond, the all-devouring
All-time champion of feeding on demand –

You want the freedom of my boyfriend's arse.
You're all over him, private jokes, the lot.

No deal. When you try to outflank me
I'll force-feed you a deep-throat dinner.

If you marched on a full stomach I'd say nothing,
But I'm scared you'll teach my pet your scrounging appetites

So hands off, while you can without a scandal –
Unless you want a mouthful that chokes you to death.

Ancestors blossom
At last in you. When you fall
All sweetness dies out,

Juventius, and I'd rather you buried him in
Great stinking piles of money
Than let him trail his ropes across your skin.
He is no Master
And he's broke.

'Why? Isn't he nice?' Oh not again.
Yes, nice enough for a man who's not a Master,
And broke.

Spin it any way you like

But he's no Master
And he's broke

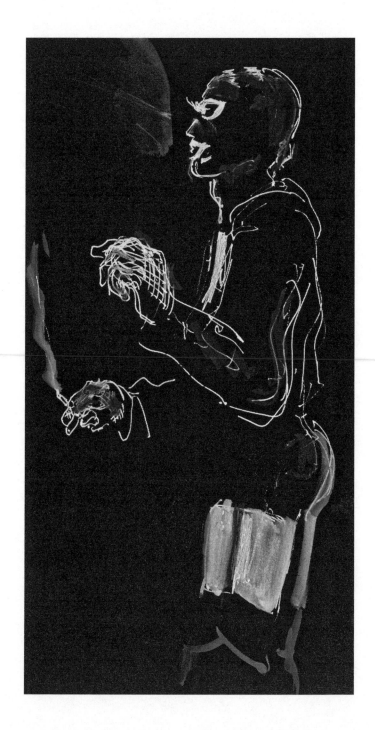

Ah! perfido

Alfenus. Stirrer, traitor, heart macerator,
False-flag planter, ironclad stone-heart bastard.
Happy now you've let me down?
No regret for my lost embrace?

Treachery won't get you likes and followers.
You left me washed up on my rocky island.
Where should the loyal long-term investor look now?

I'm mastered by your inkblot pupils spreading
As you close in for your on-centre
Perfect kiss
Cupid's bow cruelty

Then I'm blocked
Everything you did and said
Howled down by winds
Deleted from the cloud

Trade Nebulas all you want
Lashed to cryptocurrency
Facts will find you out
Holding counterfeit

It's from Catullus. *Pleeease*, he says,
Blah blah darling, you're so hot,
So talented –
He wants my after-lunch slot,

A firm booking with no one else
Looking. He says if I stay
In the camera's eye
And concentrate
He'll come nine times

In that weird way of his.
You know he calls it 'fucktuations', right?

Now it's urgent, have I got
A cancellation? He's full of carbs,
Adopting the position

And here it is.
Look away now.
The dick pic.

34

Blessed Diana's girls intact
the pregnant one sacked
school song sung lesson bells rung
Dian's bud o'er Cupid's flower
Lewis and Short avoiding sport
turn over

Oh Latona's daughter/of greatest (masculine)/
great (feminine)/progeny of Jove
whom mother/by the/pertaining to Delos/
bore (gave birth to)/olive tree

To make you mistress of the peaks
the green retreats
secret paths
laughing streams

You the virgin in the moonlight
patroness of labour pains
you the empress of the crossways
'Moon Mask' your embroidered name-tape

You presiding over sick bay's
blanketed heaps with menstrual cramps
setting rhythms that will bring un-
wasted eggs to harvest festival

Holy by what name you choose
hover as we seek to gloss
the gerund in the haunted hatband's
Serviendo crescimus

Now we turn to the Andrex annals
Scribbled by Mr Voluble –
They'll let Mistress keep her promise
To Venus and Cupid, no less.

She swears on her high-gloss pile of Taschen books
That if I come back to her bonds
And don't spike her on spondees
She'll take the juiciest chunks
By the worst poet and let the fire-god Vulcan
(How appropriate, he's lame) scorch them
In her Stefano Ferrara pizza oven.
The world's worst woman thinks it's some kind of
Joke about my selected works.

Let Venus (emerging from the pool to drip
Blessings on Araki's collectors' editions
While noting a personal preference for Sugiura)
Stamp a receipt for a smart substitution:

Here's Mr Voluble's epic crap –
Into the flames, a shoddy shitfest.

37

You boys queueing outside Berlin Berlin –
You think you're the only ones with cocks,
Let in to fuck the girls
While the rest of us get herded away?

Have another think.

*The poet fantasises about ejaculating in the reluctant faces of two
hundred male clubbers. He then considers his options.*

I'll squirt correctly spelt obscene graffiti
All over your façade

Because the girl who broke out of my hold –
Loved with more love
Than other women will reap,
The one I had such brutal fights to keep –
Is your house dominant.

They all want her, the cream of the alphas and –
Harder for me to bear – the bottom feeders

Especially *you*, lord of the hairy-arsed,
All the way from Saragossa's
Plague-zone of randy fluffy bunnies –
Señor Egnatius, raised to foreign nobility
By your clogged beard and glaring expat teeth
Scrubbed with vintage Spanish urine.

The poet puts down his tools and goes for a pee.

38

… with a murmur… my ravings…

Can't go on but does
Can't be borne but must be
Down and the weight bears down
Each day each hour Cornificius
Bad for your Catullus
But have you written the least
The tiniest scrap to calm me?
Feel my rage. Is this all your love means?

Whisper me a consolation please
Sadder than Housman's trembling tears

Mr Grey, what slip of the mind
Drove a creature like you
Into my lines?

Did you rub a genie's lamp
And wake up in this stupid fight?

You want to be talked about in the vernacular
Whatever the damage?

You will be.

You got too close to Mistress.

The term is life.

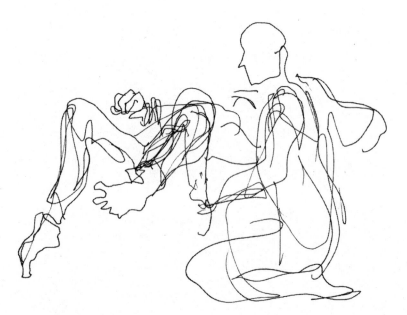

4 1

Ameana, Lady Fuck-me,
Tried to bill me for 10k –
That one with the fretwork septum
And the bankrupt beach-bum ponce.

What did Jimmy Goldsmith say?
'Beauty is a social necessity.'

Gather round and get her sectioned –
Show her what a cheap brass looks like.

I'll chuck verbiage at her,
Give it the works.
That fat slag thinks I'm a joke
And won't return my poetry notebook. Imagine!

Let's go after her and get it back.
Which one? That specimen
Waddling along with her amdram laugh.

Butcher's-dog-faced bitch. Block her path.
'Fat slag, give back his notebook!
Give him back his Moleskine, you fat slag!'

She doesn't give a toss, the dirty cow.
[Put something filthy here/leave a space]

Don't give up.
At least we'll rub her dogface in it.

So, louder:
'Fat slag, we said Moleskine, not foreskin.
Give it back, you fat slag!'

Still nothing. We'll change tactics
And get a result this time:

'Mother Superior – *s'il vous plaît* – the works?'

43

And a big Veronese hello to you, lady.
You could fix your nose hammer toes eyebags nails
Oral hygiene
Even if your tongue stays unpegged
And the bankrupt beachboy's a fixture

But back home they say you don't need any work done –
That you're Mistress's equal
[Shudders]

45

Septimius perched his girlfriend Acme
On his knee. 'Poppet,' he said,
'If I'm not properly prepared
To pine for you with desperate love,
Panting in perpetuity,
Then chop me up with pickled peppers,
Make me into vindaloo
And feed me to the lions.'

Someone dressed as Cupid did a line
From left to right and sneezed but that was fine.

Acme lightly raised her head,
Kissed her lover's pooling eyes
With scarlet lips and said, 'My darling
Septimillus, we'll stay bound
In just one service, and I'll feel it
More than you because you'll seal it
On my skin with melted wax.'

Cupid passed the kutchie on the left hand
Side and sneezed – a good omen. Bless you.

Now with coupledom's gold card,
Watch these padlocked lovebirds preening.
Poor Septimius chooses Acme,
Turns down postings (Syria, Britain).
Fixed on her Septimius,
Acme's rewarded with good kinky sex.

Who could challenge for their gleaming
His-and-hers trophy in the Venus stakes?

Cupid and my Campaspe play'd
At cards for kisses

I could have stopped there
You were the best kisser
Never needed to progress
Beyond the kissing
Only the kissing
Your soft mouth for hours forever
So stick that on your gilt-framed reproduction

But now the cherry hung with snow
Has been cut down so I must go.
I won't give a sparrow's fart
For Housman's guilt or Cupid's dart

And you'll be my Echo without knowing
I'll be closer than your gilt-flecked frosted lipstick
Kissing your words
In a scatter of sweet-coloured hundreds and thousands

Carry me across the lands and waters
For this sad rite
Hail, mortal. Hail!
So, goodnight

46

Sprung from shielding by a sigh on skin...

Pent-up stormy skies at the equinox are
Calmed by breath of a traveller's west wind.
You can leave the plains of duty, Catullus,
And the stuffy trap of productivity:
Book a one-way seat to city glitter,
Let your blanched ambition find the light,
Map the spaces where you'll dance and run.

Friends so close without touch in this ordeal – we've
Come too far from our intended roads, let's
Part and meet our freedom in scattered ways.

47

Pig. And your pig-pen friend
The Socrates wannabe –
Piso's twin left hands
Spreading virus and famine,
Nowhere out of bounds.

Did that worn-out prick
Slip you extra rations
Ahead of my own pets
Veranius and Fabullus?
You graze between meals on his massive
Stockpile while my boys
Slink to the foodbank

Let me do that
Japanese thing
Juventius
Lick your eyeball
Saliva saline
Oculus
Osculation
Ooh your big
Round O eyes
No zeros
Haven't got those
I'm kissing you
A million times better
One two three
Pass it to me
This one has lots of
Little dry seeds look
Do they pop
Never stop

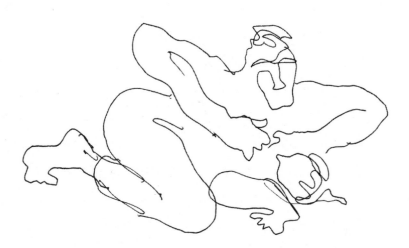

50

Yesterday we filled
A void, Licinius…

Coils to lines on skin
Coining words for torso
Torment torque torsion
Flipped the Master switch
Who'll be Torquemada?
Purple and white hide
Jute-burned scored
Red at the denouement

Now alone in the night
Too full of you to eat
No sleep to smother fires
Squirming churning the covers
Spreadeagled aching for daylight
Muscles sore nerves
Numb from the tourniquet
I will open out the book of you
Make you soar with eagles over the edge

So be meek my love and take the hurt
Which Nemesis spears through me.
She's ruthless. Don't talk back.

51

I can't compete with the rock-god superhero
God's begging him to accept the shiniest halo
That man intent on you
Ogling provoking

Your sexy laughter I'm muted
My nerves torn out with hooks
Because when I see you Clodia I
Fumble for a line and

<Find a lacuna>

Mouth crammed with earth
Limbs hot and clumsy with longing
High tide pounding my skull
Trashed headlights and a windscreen
Crazed to opacity

Idling Catullus it stalls your intention
And maidens call it love-in-idleness
Without a plan you're restless and distracted
Idle coasting toppled kings and golden
Cities in legends

Oh go ahead with giving head to the godhead
God help us he outdogs the gods of dogging
Monopolising you with his cheap tactics
Paying attention

Making you laugh and my receptors go haywire
Because one look at you Mistress and
I can't even form a polite request
For *semenawa*

My tongue dries cold blue tied to bamboo
Slung body hurts in tight jute knots
Rope burns and bare skin flinches from hot wax drips
Techno rattles my brain
Stinging eyes
Submit to the blindfold and and

Wanking, Orlando. It's unproductive.
Wanking makes you fretful and distracted.
Legendary kings and shiny cities,
Lost to wanking.

52

Still here, Catullus? Why put off the lethal dose?
Lies and cruelty are the only cards in play
With maniacs in charge and Armageddon close.
Don't hang around, Catullus. Here's the tourniquet.

56

Oh you'll love this
Bloody hilarious
Cato yes no really look at me
Don't go
Too funny
So I take some G
Sneak into the dungeon
On my own
Find a kid
Pounding some girl
I don't bother to ask
(So slap my wrist
It's a stupid rule anyway)
And make him the meat in the sandwich

Look, am I boring you or something
I bored him with this skewer lol
OK you can read it another way
It's dark and I'm dead
There was no girl
Only Mistress's boy slave

Or her brother

Beating time to thoughts of her as we do

Oh Christ look have some of this
Of course I can handle it

58

Glue. Bit.

Oh Caelius –

Mistress, Herself, her Worship, our own Lady of the
Labia, the one the poet loved
More than himself and all the rest –

Now downloadable dogging in urban areas
And choking on locally elected members

60

You got your manners from scavenging mountain lions?
Or self-aborted from Scylla's horror cave
To agitate the howling dogs lodged there?

Is that why you despise the beggar's
Plea of urgent need?

Your heat, your heart of a bitch.

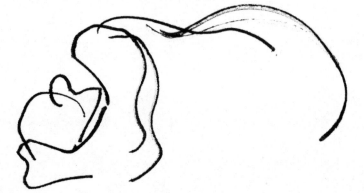

63

Attis

Superhighway vector Otis otorhinolaryngeal
Sea spray dream snow yacht lane ketamised to Anatolia

Skimming deep realities Attis scudded over water
Pierced the sunless forest rimming the home of the goddess mother
Crested a personal best of disgust mind undone
Sawed into his scrotal sac with sharp serrated stone
Felt the tag of maleness gone
Warm blood spattered on the ground
Grasped taut skin
With snowdrift hands

Your own tympanum mother and your labyrinth beyond

Pattered out a rhythm on the scraped bull's hide
And set off in the feminine
To quaver at her copyists:

'Reach for the porcelain shepherdess
On your mother's high pine shelf.
You follow my traces
Like displaced flocks
Seeking new folds in untranslated landscapes.
The sea tried to drown you in salt-eroded wrecks,
You gelded yourselves in disgust at grown-up sex –
Now make your exile fodder to amuse
Our Mistress of Dindymus and the Epididymis.

Run to her woods
Where tinnitus screeches,
The tympanum booms,
Hollow bones groan,
Hair-thrashing fangirls
Are roped with ivy
And worshippers scream
In ritual convulsions.

There in the name of the goddess her acolytes levitate –
We'll set the pace with the quickstep and Viennese waltz.'

Travesty-Attis
Reached a lacuna.
The choir of transcribers
Growled and trilled,
The tympanum buzzed,
Tinnitus whistled,
Annotators
Made for the groves.

Confused and panting like a
Recalcitrant bride, Attis
Struggled to lead the chorus
Crashing through the dark texts.
Weary they crawled at last
Into the mother's refuge.
Soothed by a tender stupor
They fell asleep without supper.

When the sun's barefaced searchlight
Purged the blank sky,
The hard ground, the harsh sea
And banished soporifics with thundering headaches,
The sleep god prodded Attis awake
And scurried off to the arms of his anxious wife.

After a night of release from bad dreams,
Bitter recall drove Attis sobbing
Back to the amniotic sea of vastness.

'Oh Mummy, oh my first home, where I was safe,
I'm so unhappy.
I ran away, as wretched as fugitive slaves,
And found the white powder mountain
Where terror crouches in frozen dens.
Mania dragged me to each dark hiding place
But Mummy I can't find you here.
I long to hold you in my gaze
For this one flicker of sanity.

Must I be cast out, give up possessions,
People who love me, places where I shine?
The clubs, the pool, the park for five-a-side?
I can't bear the pain on pain.
Is there a human part I haven't played?
Woman, man, hormonal adolescent,
Child. They eyed me at the gym, with my oiled
Torso. I had all the followers.
Every morning I woke up to streams
Of hearts and likes.
Am I now the goddess mother's full-time
Slave but just half man?

Am I washed up on a green waste
Under the jagged peaks of the frigid mountain,
Alone with the hart and the hog in the wood and the forest?
Now what I did stabs home.
Now I am punished.'

Spiralling from scarlet lips, this lament
Coiled along the goddess mother's cochleae.
She raised the yoke from her twin carriage
Dragons and flicked the nearside predator:

'Hound him back to madness and the forest
For daring to resist my domination.
Use your barbed tail for self-flagellation.
Burst eardrums. Snort red fire.' The queen of spite
Let go. The frantic monster lashed its hide,
Roared and hurtled across the smouldering scrub
To the bleached wet sands where Attis stood forlorn
On the amniotic fluid's glaring
Brink, *lŏcă lītŏrĭs.*

The dragon lunged, the manic creature plunged
Back into the scene, a submissive forever.

Goddess mother, supervisor, bitch –
Keep me free from all this lunacy, Mistress.
Let the others overdose and switch.
What I mean is, can I call you Mummy?
She called me Darling.

Floorwork

You write to me tearful castaway gasping
foam seethes drowned wreck cling neck
demand my kiss of life
goddess of sex has you wakeful
marooned on narrow mattress raging
inflamed can't be calmed by classic writers
the old reliable thumb-sucking lullabies –
I'm touched it's me you turn to
For words of consolation and love
But I'm stranded too –
No blessing left in my pockets

The minute I was legal
I dazzled, grabbed it all,
Flowers, nettles,
Pain and the pleasure of pain. The frenzy stopped
Dead with my brother's death.
Oh my brother I couldn't keep you safe
I wear black in your endless wake
Your grave our house now
The joy I rooted in your love rotten

My mind can't break for the surface.
You say I piss away time here in Verona
While the alpha male clambers on top of her
In the bed I deserted –
You misread me. Grief holds me down,
Stultifies a gift of words. No flow of writers here.

I left them in Rome; now just half a shelf.
Don't think I'm sulking or lying,
Keeping back books or love.
I'm icebound
Or I would come.

68 (B)

Eight transitions

Muses, unpeg my tongue.
Time mustn't scribble over
What Allius did for me.
I'll hold him above the dark tide
something missing/go on
The spider at work in the cornice
Won't blur his inscription with cobwebs.

You saw the hate-love torture
Cauterise me like lava
Or boiling springs,
My cheeks striated with tears,
But just as water tumbles
To relieve the parched valley
And soft breath answers storm-vexed
Prayers in the dark pumping vortex,
That's how Allius helped me –
Spreading a gangway of flowers on broad dry land
He gave us a safe house for sex
Where I waited for Mistress's
Shimmering goddess aura,
The click of heels on worn tiles.
Her threshold pause

And matching her, love-fixated
Long-dead Laodamia skirted the scaffolding
To enter the house of her bridegroom Protesilaus
(First to spring to the fight and be cut down) –
The unblessed shell unfinished like the marriage
Badly begun without blood sacrifice
(Always make me check the rubric
Before I commit) – but Laodamia learned
The altar's fascination with gore
Before she had time for enough or too much sex
With the one-day husband dragged from her arms
When the Helen grab set Greece on Troy

The deadly Middle East sump, Troy
Humanity's acrid ash, Troy
The stop to my brother's life.
These tears are for my brother taken mid-flight,
My brother, the family's best hope
Rammed in its tomb.
We died with you. Our happiness
Fed on your love's honey.
You are down with anonymous dead
In Troy's distant filth

Where the pick of the Greeks
Deserting their firesides
Pricked Paris's dream
Of wallowing with the adulteress
And widowhood took you
At beauty's peak, Laodamia.
You'd plunged to love's core –
Here's Arcadia's flood pit
Dug by Hercules mining
The soft parts beneath the mons

When man-eating birds were his bull's-eyes
And he was a king's slave
Parting heaven's gates
To marry the goddess of being young

But your love bored deeper than this.
Tamed by dominance
You loved him more than the rich man loves his grandchild
Born in time to disinherit the distant
Relative poised like a comedy vulture –
More than the frantic snowy dove
Adores the mate she pecks in a kissing frenzy –
Your headlong passion outstripped theirs
As you clung to your blond hero

And with desire as fierce as yours – possibly –
Mistress came to me burnished
With Cupid's saffron glow.
She isn't satisfied with just the one
Catullus of course
Among her (few) conspirators.
In her position one doesn't bestow
Exclusivity
But it would be otiose to object –
Watch me, I'm Juno, queen of heaven,
Holding the lid on her boiling rage
While Jupiter puts it about…
Not that it's OK to compare gods with mortals
the connection was lost here/no it wasn't
Don't harp on like a doddery parent – it's thankless.
And she wasn't exactly given away to me
By a doting father in front of

Scented lilies in serried arrangements,
But on a night of miracles
She smuggled in what scraps she could offer stolen
From an actual husband's actual bed.
It's enough if she weighs her hours with me like diamonds

So, Allius, for services rendered
Take a home-made poem to rust-proof your name.
Be happy, you and your woman,
The house where we could play at being married
this bit's rusty/drop it
And far above everyone else
The woman who casts the light.
I love her more than life, I live
Through her, touch happiness through her.

70

She says she wouldn't marry
Anyone but me
Even if God Almighty
Got down on one knee.

Her words. But what a woman
Tells a rampant lover
Scrolls out on the wind
And the swollen river.

72

When I saw everything through gauze
You said 'I'm yours' and made me king.
I prized you – not just as a male
Grabs his polyester bride
But as a lion loves his pride.

Now I see with unstreaked eyes,
Your squalid lies turn up the flame.
You ask 'How come?' *As if you didn't* –
Because the talons in the wound
Make the lover more feverish, less kind.

They won't break your fall but they smash up everything else.
They let your harness slip so you hang by your neck –
All of them, all of the time.

Your generous acts get spat right back.
They cut you down to smack the floor with your face.

Take my case.
The one who got the gold for cruelty
And put my life in a choke-hold
Had said, 'No one but you. My only friend.'

75

This is what we've come to, Clodia. My
Self-will has been dragged down by the beast in you and
Drowned in its own pool of meaning well.

I couldn't bring myself to like you now
Even if you played the convent girl

Or give up loving you, no matter how
Wide you spread your legs to the whole world.

Intra-Venus

What does being honest feel like?
If you keep a faithful note
Of how you avoid the crooked route,
There's comfort when your hair's gone white
[Don't bother, you won't make it – Ed.]
Salvaged from this obsessive blight.

What altruism says or does,
You've said, done, and been called
A prick for it. Accept the pain.
The vein's collapsed. Rip out the line.

It's hard to abandon a love that runs a life

But hanging on will hurt you more.
Here are twelve steps and a door.

If anyone knows what pity is, if you've waltzed
Someone away from the edge,
Watch me – and if you see gold in my sad river,
Save me from being a burning, boring addict.

My love is not reflected in her eyes.
Ask her where she's been and she tells lies.
I want to be released from this
Corrosive habit.
I had integrity. Please.

77

Well, Captain Scarlet.
That went nowhere, our zero-sum game.
It was looking like friendship from here.

Did I say nowhere? Here's my heart crashing
Into the red, hijacked by grief.

Was this your plan – play the blood-brother,
Barbecue my certainties to a *saignant* crimson,

Do your superhero swoop
To grab it all out of my arms?

You stole my life.

I weep for how you seeded my arteries,
Weep for our closeness that came with a fatal condition.

79

Brother/switch
Sister/bitch
Pretty Clodius is the catch
So Clodia will hitch him close,
Cut loose the poet and his rope family –

But let Sir Pretty of the Clan McPretty
Give those rope orphans to unattractive Masters
If he can beg three single-column ties
Eins zwei drei
From those who know what he plies

Couldn't you find a decent rigger, Juventius,
Instead of the spray-tanned poser from Watford
Who's binding you now? How dare you prefer
His ropes to mine?
You don't know
How stupid you look, dangling and spinning like that.

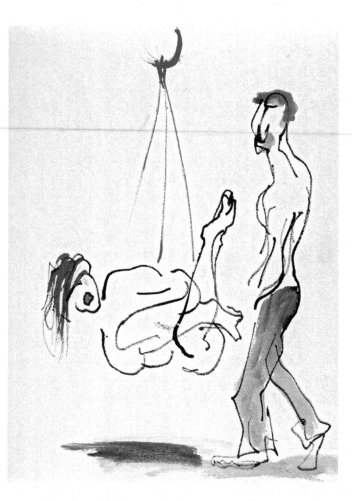

82

Look at me, Quintius.

If you want me to believe
I'd sacrifice my eyesight for your sake,
Or something even more precious than these eyes,

Don't force us apart.

Believe I love her more than I love these eyes,
More than I love the gifts more precious than sight.

Clodia lingers over all my faults
For hubby's benefit. He laps it up.

Twat. Cat got your brain?

If she could blot out what we share
Shut that mouth
She'd be over it

But her epic monologue
Is a mnemonic
For me

And worse than that to goad her on

The needle in the skin
Concentrated acid on the tongue

'a pleasantly trivial anecdote ridiculing the pretensions of an upstart'
– The Oxford Anthology of Roman Literature (OUP)

Haspirations, says 'Arry.
He's got plenty of those,
All that gusty huffing –
Fighting with bows and harrows
Makes his ardour harder.

Gets it from his mother
And jumped-up hancestors
With hairs instead of heirs.

How our ears rejoiced
At his posting overseas
Then closed up with distaste
When we heard about Haitch R Haitch –

Wipe that look off your face.
This pleasant enough for you?
Were you at the other place?

85

Odi et amo. quare id faciam, fortasse requiris?
nescio, sed fieri sentio et excrucior.

Hate I/hating I and love I/loving I. By what thing it do I/doing
I perhaps enquire you/enquiring you

Not know I/not knowing I but to happen/to be happening feel I/
feeling I and tortured I/tortured I am being

I hate where I do love. Perchance
Thou seek'st to know *de quelle façon*
[Doffs hat, strums lute-strings].
I don't know. It's hurting. *Here.*

Hate-love-hate-love you ask why the needle's stuck
I can't say but the pain is an endless track

HATE/LOVE. Since you've got to ask –
Me neither. But [because?] it's torture.

I'm in love with loathing. You demand reasons
I can't give. But they're real, the hooks in my flesh.

Attraction-repulsion. You shove your probe right in.
[shrug] It's a vocation, having my liver plucked out.

Stuck in a hate-love trap.
'How does it make you feel?'
Don't give me that counselling crap.
The wheel has spikes. Bones snap.

86

And *that's* supposed to be beautiful –
Pulling the milkshake limbs out straight and long.
Boring.
You get points for technique
But they don't add up to beauty.

Your bland suspension
Has no magic,
No pinch of suffering passivity,
No hurt, no sweat.

Now look at mine.
There's blinding beauty in that tie,
More than yours or anybody's,
Executed with tricks I took from the best.

87

No woman can attest that she
Is in receipt of love to the degree
Assigned to Lesbia by me

No contract holds as tightly as the force of
Love that binds me to your claws

No, Gellius.
That's not why I hoped you'd stay onside
In my pitiful, pitiless affair.
It wasn't my X-ray eyes, or trust, or believing
That you could keep your mind off sex for a second –

No. It was because she wasn't your mother.
Or your sister.

My love for her gnawed like cancer.

I thought the fact that you and I were friends
Wouldn't be enough to unbind your hands.
And look what happened. You love to boost your frail
Member in the compost of betrayal.

92

Clodia slanders me on oath
Can't be forced to shut her mouth
So Clodia loves me *by Almighty
God.* What is the proof? I'm just the
Same – I'd string her up but I'm
In love with her *whole truth and nothing*

93

Trinidadian Creole by Jason Anthony Henry

Caesar yuh see me, I doh have time fuh you an dis set ah
bacchanal nah. If yuh like me den dat good, if not well dah is
you. Whether yuh white or yuh black is de same khaki pants.

93

And your mother

I can't be arsed to please you, Caesar.
Your hide could be white or black for all I care.

Microsoft Outlook

⚠ GV Catullus requested a read receipt be sent
when message 'And your mother' is read.
Do you want to send a receipt?

☐ Don't ask me about sending receipts again.

[Yes]   [No]

96

If the silent coffin space
Can find sustenance
In our grief, Calvus, which shares a seam
Of longing with loves we once
Knew and need to feel again
And with tears we cry
For deep commitment cast away,
Quintilia does not grieve
Her death that was too soon but lies
Enraptured by your love.

99

I couldn't stop myself
You were helpless in my ropes
The smell of you
Juventius listen
It was the best

But I didn't get away with it.
You hauled me up and strung me out
Inverted crucifix
For more than sixty minutes.
I sobbed and said sorry
But you left me transfixed.

I'd barely untied you
Before you ran to wash yourself
And flicked away the water with your delicate hands
Scared I'd infect you
With crack-whore juice.

You sacrificed me to your fury
Spatchcocked
And reconditioned my reflex
To make that moment more explosive than
The world's worst emetic.

If this is your revenge on a hard Master
I'll never help myself again.

Verona's hottest boys
Scouting for new owners
Score a sibling act.
Caelius picks the brother,
Quintius the other –
Cute fraternal pact.

Which one gets the kudos?
Caelius, it's you –
Bonded as we are,
Hardened in the fire
When that Mistress phase
Torched my sanity.
Caelius, stay lucky,
Beat the casino at love.

101

Flight-shamed through the earthbound ports and checkpoints
I'm here, brother, for this bleak ceremony,
To help you fathom death's assembly kit
And offer useless words to wordless ashes.
I wasn't strong enough to keep hold of you.
Now I'll never find the missing piece

Here are the conventional sad tokens
For the old rituals that told us so.
Take them sea-splashed with a brother's tears
And for ever like the tide, my brother,
I come to claim you and to let you go

103

Be so gracious as to
Give back that 10k
I paid for shoddy leaky
Girlfriends for the night,
Silo, and enjoy
Your vicious thug life –

Or if you'd rather shag the
Cash then be my guest but
Don't be a vicious thug
Pimp.

104

You think I cursed the woman
More central to me than my brain stem?

If I could reach so low
I wouldn't be lost in trackless love for her.

You bastards want to pull down all the cathedrals.

Breaking

If the single object of hope and longing
Can be possessed with the snap of a wishbone it's...

Welcome.
Welcome back. You're what I've longed for,
More than the big cash prize, and you've *come back,*
Clodia, come back to me on a bone's crack,

I've longed for

Back

Oh this is a day of delirium.
Who's happier than I am? Who can think
That I'll have any further need for hope?

Lockdown

Our special place.
Yes Mistress.
You're dangling
Our love affair
As a fixture, you and me, I can nearly –

Please Mistress

No mistrust. Make her mean it
Straight from the heart with no slick coating
So that we can formalise the thing
In a mystic tantric bond of transcendental –

Yes Mistress

34

Serviendo crescimus (in service we grow) was the motto of Woking Girls' Grammar School.

38

This might be Quintus Cornificius, poet and military commander, who left one fragment of poetry:

deducta mihi voce garrienti
subdued/(to?) me/voice/chattering

45

References to Britain and Syria suggest that this poem might have been written towards the end of Catullus's life.

Cupid and my Campaspe play'd
At cards for kisses
is the beginning of a poem by John Lyly (1553–1606).

A.E. Housman wrote:
About the woodlands I will go
To see the cherry hung with snow.

The last two lines of this version are fairy words from *A Midsummer Night's Dream*.

46

'Shielding' has come to mean 'staying at home for health reasons during a pandemic'.

51

There is a line missing from the original, where shown
in hairpins (page 47); it has the same metre as 'scholarly
guesswork'. Catullus's first three stanzas are a translation of
Sappho 31.

'And maidens call it love-in-idleness' are Oberon's words in *A
Midsummer Night's Dream*.

56

Alternative readings make the event obscure so I offer three
versions.

79

The family name of Clodia and her brother Clodius was
Pulcher (handsome).

81

Catullus takes a metropolitan swipe at Pisaurum, now Pesaro
and twinned with Watford.

I find a two-term weekly class on Catullus textual criticism. I email Stephen Harrison, Professor of Latin Literature at Oxford. May I attend as a graduate of this establishment? 'It's rather austere,' he warns. But I would like to peer at the living conjecture about what Catullus wrote.

His works survive through one incomplete manuscript, shot with mistakes (not his), which bobbed up in about 1300, was copied, and vanished again. Since the Renaissance a stream of scholars, including A.E. Housman, have been on the unachievable quest for authenticity.

One fourteenth-century scribe was so concerned about the wretched state of the material that he wrote a note (in the third person) asking for the reader's pardon: '... in order to assemble something from this rough and ready source, he decided that it was better to have it in a corrupt state than not to have it at all, while hoping still to be able to correct it from

67 6 DUCTA

CO

another copy which might happen to emerge. Fare you well, if you do not curse him.'

That translation from the Renaissance Latin is by Professor Harrison.[1] Subtly hand-jiving fragments of the poems, he runs the class jointly with Professor Stephen Heyworth.

Today Dr Tristan Franklinos canters through the variants in poem 69. For example, the third line begins with a meaningless *nos illa mare* (we or us/her or that/sea) found in the three oldest surviving manuscripts. They are in the Bodleian Library in Oxford, the Bibliothèque nationale de France and the Biblioteca Apostolica Vaticana.

Contenders include the widely accepted Renaissance version *non si illam **rarae*** (not if...her...fine...), *non si illam **carae*** (expensive), and *non si illam **Coae*** (of a female prostitute or of the Coan moth – that is, fine silk). With the rest of the line it could mean: 'Even if you try to seduce her with pricey labels...'

Like a successful virus, a single corrupted anthology, emanating by chance, continues to be replicated and is improved in the process. As centuries pass it becomes more or less widespread according to the cultural climate.

Time longer than rope
       – Jamaican proverb

---

1   'The Need for a New Text of Catullus' in *Vom Text zum Buch*, ed. C. Reitz (St Katharinen, 2001), 63–79.

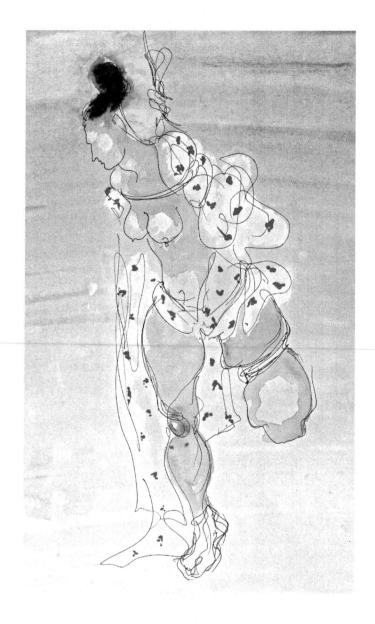

Theresa May pleaded with Conservative MPs on Monday not to tie her hands in Brexit negotiations in Brussels, as party whips hoped they had bought off Tory rebels ahead of 48 hours of potentially knife-edge votes in the House of Commons.

Financial Times, 12 June 2018

During his absence I had not been unhappy. Being invited to other people's houses had given me a feeling of superiority, as I compared their insipidly pleasant state to my own. There was a barrier between them and me, invisible but impassable like the invisible bars in modern zoos, where the tropical animals are confined within their ground by a space of heated air.

At the same time, I knew that they in turn would have been uncomprehending if they had known that my contentment came from a man who was able to say, 'I shall hold you for ever, because I shall always find new ways of torturing you,' and that my own particular paradise of the green fitted carpet, the blond machine-carved furniture, and the pressed-glass vases was paradise only because I did not dwell there of my own free will but was held in bondage there.

Edith Templeton, *Gordon*, Olympia Press, 1966

Oh bondage, up yours!
Oh bondage, no more!
                    Poly Styrene for X-Ray Spex, 1977

TITANIA:
Come, wait upon him; lead him to my bower.
The moon, methinks, looks with a watery eye,
And when she weeps, weeps every little flower,
Lamenting some enforced chastity.
Tie up my love's tongue, bring him silently.
        Shakespeare, *A Midsummer Night's Dream*

Whatever diminishes constraint, diminishes strength. The
more constraints one imposes, the more one frees one's self of
the chains that shackle the spirit.
        Igor Stravinsky, *Poetics of Music in the Form of Six Lessons*,
        translated by Arthur Knodel and Ingolf Dahl, Harvard
        University Press, 1947

The Bracelet: to Julia
Why I tie about thy wrist,
Julia, this silken twist;
For what other reason is't
But to show thee how, in part,
Thou my pretty captive art?
But thy bond-slave is my heart:

'Tis but silk that bindeth thee,
Knap the thread and thou art free;
But 'tis otherwise with me:
I am bound and fast bound, so
That from thee I cannot go;
If I could, I would not so.
        Robert Herrick (1591–1674)

Round field hedge now flowers in full glory twine
Large bindweed bells wild hop and streakd woodbine
John Clare, *The Shepherd's Calendar – June*, 1827

Unwilling lovers, love doth more torment
Than such as in their bondage feel content.
Lo I confess, I am thy captive I,
And hold my conquered hands for thee to tie.
Ovid, *Amores* 1.2, translated by Christopher Marlowe

There was a sharp burning pain in my groin, where my harness was digging in under tension. The ropes were tangled round my body. Above me they stretched in a tight line towards dark rocks. I tried craning my neck to look up but could distinguish no human shapes – just a slender thread attached miraculously to something on the mountain. There was still no sound – just a bleak, grey emptiness. I seemed to be suspended in some gloomy limbo, alone and deserted. I wondered whether the others had been pulled off – whether they were all dead, or unconscious from terrible injuries, powerless to rescue me from this overwhelming sense of abandonment.

Stephen Venables, *A Slender Thread*, Hutchinson, 2000

November 21.

My Nightmare

There is always something which drags me back from the achievement of my desires. It's like a nightmare; I see myself struggling violently to escape from a monster which draws continuously nearer, until his shadow falls across my path, when I begin to run and find my legs tied, etc. The only difference is that mine is a nightmare from which I never wake up. The haven of successful accomplishment remains as far off as ever. Oh! make haste.

W.N.P. Barbellion, *The Journal of a Disappointed Man*, G.H. Doran, 1919

And every poet has some Muse from whom he is suspended, and by whom he is said to be possessed, which is nearly the same thing; for he is taken hold of.

Plato, *Ion*, translated by Benjamin Jowett, 1871

A thin karmic thread winds between us, linking us through something the poem holds that is true to this moment. But a karmic bond that consists of such a very tenuous thread is scarcely, after all, a burdensome matter. Nor is it any ordinary thread – it is like some rainbow arching in the sky, a mist that trails over the plain, a spider's web glittering in the dew, a fragile thing that, though marvellously beautiful to the eye, must snap at the first touch. What if this thread were to swell before my eyes into the sturdy thickness of a rope? I wonder. But there's no danger of this. I am an artist. And she is far from the common run of woman.

Natsume Sōseki, *Kusamakura*, 1906, translated by Meredith McKinney, Penguin Classics, 2008

GARDENER:
Go bind thou up young dangling apricocks
Shakespeare, *Richard II*

Models and riggers: Unnamed; Miss Bones (model) and Fred Hatt (rigger), page 16, page 94; Cad and Phoenix Flight, page 64, page 69; Denisse, Whiterabbit and Udo, cover, title page, page 52, page 65, page 75, page 88; Gorgone and Nina Russ, opposite Shibari Carmina 'instructions'; Isabelle Hanikamu and Koikunawa, page 93; O.c. Harddwn and Fred Rx, page 98; MaYa Homerton and Miss Eris, page 8 (lower); Ada La Venom and Osada Steve, page 6, page 8 (upper), page 13; Ayumi LaNoire, page 24; Federica Laquartacorda and Andrea Quartacorda, page 40; Niyouli and Yoroï Nicolas, page 85; Kitty Rea and Maxim Kalahari, page 39; Kitty Rea and Nina Russ, opposite Propertius epigraph, also page 58; Sasha and Gestalta, page 22; Skinny Red Art, page 71; Tenshiko and Kirigami, page 10; Zlata and Red Lily, page 21, page 96.

With thanks to Nina and Aidan – BiZarre Events London (page 29, page 33).

CAUTION

Please do not try shibari without instruction.

TRAINING

anatomiestudio.com (Anna Bones and Fred Hatt)
laquartacorda.it/en/nawame (Andrea Quartacorda)
Oxford Rope Bight (Phoenix Flight and others/FetLife)
shibariclasses.com (Nina Russ and Bruce Esinem)
shibaristudy.com (Gorgone and others)
studiokokoro.co.uk, wykd.com (Clover and Wykd Dave)
yoroi-dojo.org (Yoroï Nicolas)